50 Summer BBQ Recipes: Grilling Favorites for Hot Days

By: Kelly Johnson

Table of Contents

- Grilled Chicken Skewers
- BBQ Ribs
- Burgers with Classic Toppings
- Grilled Shrimp Tacos
- Vegetable Kebabs
- Hot Dogs with Assorted Condiments
- Grilled Corn on the Cob
- Lemon Herb Grilled Salmon
- Spicy Sausage and Peppers
- Grilled Portobello Mushrooms
- Marinated Flank Steak
- Grilled Pineapple with Honey
- BBQ Chicken Wings
- Stuffed Bell Peppers
- Grilled Asparagus with Balsamic Glaze
- Marinated Veggie Burgers
- Smoky BBQ Pulled Pork Sandwiches
- Grilled Zucchini and Squash
- Grilled Eggplant Parmesan
- BBQ Chicken Pizza
- Cilantro Lime Grilled Shrimp
- Grilled Flatbreads with Toppings
- Mediterranean Grilled Chicken
- Grilled Fish Tacos with Slaw
- Spicy Grilled Cauliflower Steaks
- BBQ Meatball Sliders
- Grilled Watermelon Salad
- Grilled Stuffed Peppers
- Caribbean Jerk Chicken
- Smoky BBQ Beans
- Grilled Shrimp and Vegetable Skewers
- BBQ Chicken Salad
- Honey Glazed Grilled Carrots
- Grilled Lobster Tails
- Chipotle Lime Grilled Corn
- BBQ Brisket

- Grilled Pesto Chicken
- Summer Vegetable Platter
- Grilled Sweet Potatoes
- Honey Mustard Grilled Chicken
- Margherita Grilled Pizza
- Teriyaki Grilled Chicken
- Grilled Lemon Herb Potatoes
- BBQ Cauliflower Bites
- Grilled Fruit Salad
- Shrimp and Andouille Sausage Skewers
- BBQ Chicken Nachos
- Grilled Fajitas
- Grilled Honey Garlic Shrimp
- BBQ Steak Salad

Grilled Chicken Skewers

Ingredients:

- **1 pound** boneless, skinless chicken breasts, cut into 1-inch cubes
- **1/4 cup** olive oil
- **2 tablespoons** soy sauce
- **2 tablespoons** lemon juice
- **2 cloves** garlic, minced
- **1 teaspoon** paprika
- **Salt and pepper** to taste
- **Skewers** (wooden or metal)

Instructions:

1. In a bowl, whisk together olive oil, soy sauce, lemon juice, garlic, paprika, salt, and pepper.
2. Add the chicken cubes to the marinade and toss to coat. Cover and refrigerate for at least 30 minutes.
3. Preheat the grill to medium-high heat. Thread the marinated chicken onto skewers.
4. Grill the skewers for about 10-12 minutes, turning occasionally, until the chicken is cooked through and reaches an internal temperature of 165°F (75°C). Serve hot.

BBQ Ribs

Ingredients:

- **2 pounds** baby back ribs
- **1 cup** BBQ sauce (your choice)
- **Salt and pepper** to taste
- **1 teaspoon** smoked paprika (optional)

Instructions:

1. Preheat the grill to medium heat.
2. Season the ribs with salt, pepper, and smoked paprika. Place the ribs on the grill, bone side down.
3. Cover and cook for 2-3 hours, basting with BBQ sauce every 30 minutes.
4. When the ribs are tender, remove them from the grill and brush with additional BBQ sauce. Let rest for 10 minutes before slicing and serving.

Burgers with Classic Toppings

Ingredients:

- **1 pound** ground beef (80/20 blend recommended)
- **Salt and pepper** to taste
- **4 hamburger buns**
- **Lettuce, tomato, onion, pickles, cheese** (for toppings)
- **Ketchup, mustard, mayo** (for condiments)

Instructions:

1. Preheat the grill to medium-high heat.
2. Shape the ground beef into 4 patties and season with salt and pepper.
3. Grill the burgers for 4-5 minutes per side, or until they reach your desired doneness (160°F/70°C for medium).
4. Toast the buns on the grill if desired. Assemble burgers with your choice of toppings and condiments.

Grilled Shrimp Tacos

Ingredients:

- **1 pound** shrimp, peeled and deveined
- **2 tablespoons** olive oil
- **1 tablespoon** lime juice
- **1 teaspoon** chili powder
- **Salt and pepper** to taste
- **8 small corn tortillas**
- **Cabbage, avocado, salsa, lime wedges** (for serving)

Instructions:

1. In a bowl, combine shrimp, olive oil, lime juice, chili powder, salt, and pepper. Toss to coat.
2. Preheat the grill to medium-high heat. Thread the shrimp onto skewers.
3. Grill the shrimp for 2-3 minutes per side, or until they are pink and opaque.
4. Warm the tortillas on the grill. Serve the shrimp in tortillas with cabbage, avocado, salsa, and lime wedges.

Vegetable Kebabs

Ingredients:

- **1 bell pepper**, cut into chunks
- **1 zucchini**, sliced
- **1 red onion**, cut into wedges
- **8 oz** mushrooms, halved
- **1/4 cup** olive oil
- **2 tablespoons** balsamic vinegar
- **Salt and pepper** to taste
- **Skewers** (wooden or metal)

Instructions:

1. In a bowl, whisk together olive oil, balsamic vinegar, salt, and pepper.
2. Add the vegetables to the marinade and toss to coat. Let sit for at least 15 minutes.
3. Preheat the grill to medium heat. Thread the marinated vegetables onto skewers.
4. Grill for about 10-12 minutes, turning occasionally, until the vegetables are tender and slightly charred.

Hot Dogs with Assorted Condiments

Ingredients:

- **8 hot dogs**
- **8 hot dog buns**
- **Assorted condiments** (ketchup, mustard, relish, onions, sauerkraut)

Instructions:

1. Preheat the grill to medium heat.
2. Place hot dogs on the grill and cook for about 5-7 minutes, turning occasionally, until heated through and grill marks appear.
3. Toast the buns on the grill if desired. Serve hot dogs in buns with your choice of condiments.

Grilled Corn on the Cob

Ingredients:

- **4 ears** of corn, husked
- **Butter**, for serving
- **Salt** to taste

Instructions:

1. Preheat the grill to medium-high heat.
2. Wrap each ear of corn in aluminum foil and place on the grill.
3. Grill for about 15-20 minutes, turning occasionally, until tender.
4. Carefully unwrap the foil and serve the corn hot with butter and salt.

Lemon Herb Grilled Salmon

Ingredients:

- **4 salmon fillets**
- **1/4 cup** olive oil
- **2 tablespoons** lemon juice
- **1 teaspoon** dried oregano
- **1 teaspoon** garlic powder
- **Salt and pepper** to taste
- **Lemon slices** (for garnish)

Instructions:

1. In a bowl, whisk together olive oil, lemon juice, oregano, garlic powder, salt, and pepper.
2. Marinate the salmon fillets in the mixture for at least 15 minutes.
3. Preheat the grill to medium heat. Place the salmon skin-side down on the grill.
4. Grill for about 6-8 minutes per side, or until the salmon flakes easily with a fork. Garnish with lemon slices before serving.

Spicy Sausage and Peppers

Ingredients:

- **1 pound** spicy Italian sausage
- **1 bell pepper**, sliced
- **1 onion**, sliced
- **2 tablespoons** olive oil
- **1 teaspoon** Italian seasoning
- **Salt and pepper** to taste
- **Crusty bread** (for serving, optional)

Instructions:

1. Preheat the grill to medium heat.
2. In a large bowl, combine the bell pepper, onion, olive oil, Italian seasoning, salt, and pepper.
3. Grill the sausage for about 12-15 minutes, turning occasionally, until cooked through and browned.
4. In the last 5-7 minutes of cooking, add the seasoned peppers and onions to the grill. Cook until tender and slightly charred.
5. Serve the grilled sausage with the peppers and onions on crusty bread if desired.

Grilled Portobello Mushrooms

Ingredients:

- **4 large** Portobello mushrooms, stems removed
- **1/4 cup** balsamic vinegar
- **2 tablespoons** olive oil
- **2 cloves** garlic, minced
- **Salt and pepper** to taste
- **Fresh basil** (for garnish)

Instructions:

1. In a bowl, whisk together balsamic vinegar, olive oil, garlic, salt, and pepper.
2. Marinate the Portobello mushrooms in the mixture for at least 30 minutes.
3. Preheat the grill to medium-high heat. Grill the mushrooms for about 5-7 minutes per side, or until tender and grill marks appear.
4. Garnish with fresh basil before serving.

Marinated Flank Steak

Ingredients:

- **1 pound** flank steak
- **1/4 cup** soy sauce
- **2 tablespoons** olive oil
- **2 tablespoons** red wine vinegar
- **2 cloves** garlic, minced
- **1 teaspoon** black pepper
- **1 teaspoon** dried rosemary

Instructions:

1. In a bowl, whisk together soy sauce, olive oil, red wine vinegar, garlic, black pepper, and rosemary.
2. Place the flank steak in a resealable plastic bag and pour the marinade over it. Seal and refrigerate for at least 2 hours (or overnight for best results).
3. Preheat the grill to high heat. Grill the flank steak for 5-7 minutes per side, or until it reaches desired doneness.
4. Let rest for 5 minutes before slicing against the grain.

Grilled Pineapple with Honey

Ingredients:

- **1 fresh pineapple**, peeled, cored, and sliced into rings
- **2 tablespoons** honey
- **1 teaspoon** cinnamon (optional)

Instructions:

1. Preheat the grill to medium heat.
2. Brush the pineapple slices with honey and sprinkle with cinnamon if desired.
3. Grill the pineapple for about 3-4 minutes per side, or until caramelized and grill marks appear.
4. Serve warm as a dessert or side dish.

BBQ Chicken Wings

Ingredients:

- **2 pounds** chicken wings
- **1 cup** BBQ sauce (your choice)
- **Salt and pepper** to taste

Instructions:

1. Preheat the grill to medium heat.
2. Season the chicken wings with salt and pepper.
3. Grill the wings for about 20-25 minutes, turning occasionally, until cooked through and crispy.
4. Brush with BBQ sauce during the last few minutes of grilling. Serve hot with extra sauce on the side.

Stuffed Bell Peppers

Ingredients:

- **4 bell peppers**, halved and seeds removed
- **1 cup** cooked rice
- **1 pound** ground beef or turkey
- **1 cup** diced tomatoes
- **1 teaspoon** Italian seasoning
- **Salt and pepper** to taste
- **1 cup** shredded cheese (for topping)

Instructions:

1. Preheat the grill to medium heat.
2. In a skillet, cook the ground beef or turkey over medium heat until browned. Stir in the cooked rice, diced tomatoes, Italian seasoning, salt, and pepper.
3. Fill each bell pepper half with the meat and rice mixture. Top with shredded cheese.
4. Wrap each stuffed pepper in aluminum foil and grill for about 30-35 minutes, or until the peppers are tender and cheese is melted.

Grilled Asparagus with Balsamic Glaze

Ingredients:

- **1 pound** asparagus, trimmed
- **2 tablespoons** olive oil
- **Salt and pepper** to taste
- **1/4 cup** balsamic glaze

Instructions:

1. Preheat the grill to medium-high heat.
2. Toss the asparagus with olive oil, salt, and pepper.
3. Grill the asparagus for about 5-7 minutes, turning occasionally, until tender and slightly charred.
4. Drizzle with balsamic glaze before serving.

Marinated Veggie Burgers

Ingredients:

- **4 veggie burger patties**
- **1/4 cup** olive oil
- **2 tablespoons** soy sauce
- **1 tablespoon** lemon juice
- **1 teaspoon** garlic powder
- **Salt and pepper** to taste

Instructions:

1. In a bowl, whisk together olive oil, soy sauce, lemon juice, garlic powder, salt, and pepper.
2. Marinate the veggie burger patties in the mixture for at least 30 minutes.
3. Preheat the grill to medium heat. Grill the patties for about 5-7 minutes per side, or until heated through and grill marks appear.
4. Serve on buns with your choice of toppings.

Smoky BBQ Pulled Pork Sandwiches

Ingredients:

- **2 pounds** pork shoulder
- **1 tablespoon** smoked paprika
- **1 tablespoon** garlic powder
- **1 tablespoon** onion powder
- **1 teaspoon** salt
- **1 teaspoon** black pepper
- **1 cup** BBQ sauce
- **4 sandwich buns**
- **Coleslaw** (for topping, optional)

Instructions:

1. In a small bowl, mix smoked paprika, garlic powder, onion powder, salt, and pepper. Rub this mixture all over the pork shoulder.
2. Preheat the grill to indirect medium heat. Place the pork on the grill and cook for about 4-5 hours, or until tender and easily shredded.
3. Once cooked, remove the pork from the grill and shred with two forks. Mix with BBQ sauce.
4. Serve on sandwich buns and top with coleslaw if desired.

Grilled Zucchini and Squash

Ingredients:

- **2 zucchinis**, sliced
- **2 yellow squashes**, sliced
- **2 tablespoons** olive oil
- **1 teaspoon** Italian seasoning
- **Salt and pepper** to taste

Instructions:

1. Preheat the grill to medium heat.
2. In a bowl, toss the zucchini and squash slices with olive oil, Italian seasoning, salt, and pepper.
3. Grill the vegetables for about 4-5 minutes per side, or until tender and grill marks appear.
4. Serve warm as a side dish.

Grilled Eggplant Parmesan

Ingredients:

- **2 medium eggplants**, sliced into 1/2-inch rounds
- **1/4 cup** olive oil
- **1 cup** marinara sauce
- **2 cups** shredded mozzarella cheese
- **1/2 cup** grated Parmesan cheese
- **Salt and pepper** to taste
- **Fresh basil** (for garnish)

Instructions:

1. Preheat the grill to medium heat.
2. Brush the eggplant slices with olive oil and season with salt and pepper.
3. Grill the eggplant for about 4-5 minutes per side until tender and charred.
4. In a baking dish, layer grilled eggplant, marinara sauce, and mozzarella cheese. Repeat layers and top with Parmesan cheese.
5. Cover the dish with foil and grill for about 15 minutes until the cheese is melted. Garnish with fresh basil before serving.

BBQ Chicken Pizza

Ingredients:

- **1 pre-made pizza crust**
- **1 cup** cooked chicken, shredded
- **1/2 cup** BBQ sauce
- **1 cup** shredded mozzarella cheese
- **1/4 cup** red onion, thinly sliced
- **1/4 cup** cilantro, chopped (for garnish)

Instructions:

1. Preheat the grill to medium-high heat.
2. In a bowl, mix the shredded chicken with BBQ sauce.
3. Roll out the pizza crust and place it on a lightly oiled grill pan. Grill for about 2-3 minutes on one side until lightly charred.
4. Flip the crust, then top with BBQ chicken, mozzarella cheese, and red onion. Grill for an additional 5-7 minutes until the cheese is melted and bubbly.
5. Garnish with cilantro before serving.

Cilantro Lime Grilled Shrimp

Ingredients:

- **1 pound** shrimp, peeled and deveined
- **1/4 cup** olive oil
- **2 tablespoons** lime juice
- **2 tablespoons** fresh cilantro, chopped
- **1 teaspoon** garlic powder
- **Salt and pepper** to taste

Instructions:

1. In a bowl, whisk together olive oil, lime juice, cilantro, garlic powder, salt, and pepper.
2. Add shrimp to the marinade and let sit for 15-30 minutes.
3. Preheat the grill to medium-high heat. Thread shrimp onto skewers and grill for about 2-3 minutes per side until pink and cooked through.
4. Serve immediately with additional lime wedges.

Grilled Flatbreads with Toppings

Ingredients:

- **4 pre-made flatbreads**
- **1 cup** hummus or pesto (for spreading)
- **1 cup** cherry tomatoes, halved
- **1 cup** spinach leaves
- **1 cup** feta cheese, crumbled
- **Olive oil** (for brushing)

Instructions:

1. Preheat the grill to medium heat.
2. Brush one side of the flatbreads with olive oil. Place the oiled side down on the grill for about 1-2 minutes until grill marks appear.
3. Flip the flatbreads and spread hummus or pesto on top. Add cherry tomatoes, spinach, and feta cheese.
4. Close the grill lid and cook for another 3-4 minutes until the toppings are warm and the cheese is slightly melted.
5. Cut into wedges and serve warm.

Mediterranean Grilled Chicken

Ingredients:

- **4 boneless, skinless chicken breasts**
- **1/4 cup** olive oil
- **2 tablespoons** lemon juice
- **2 teaspoons** dried oregano
- **2 cloves** garlic, minced
- **Salt and pepper** to taste

Instructions:

1. In a bowl, whisk together olive oil, lemon juice, oregano, garlic, salt, and pepper.
2. Marinate the chicken breasts in the mixture for at least 30 minutes.
3. Preheat the grill to medium-high heat. Grill the chicken for about 6-7 minutes per side, or until cooked through and juices run clear.
4. Let rest for a few minutes before slicing and serving.

Grilled Fish Tacos with Slaw

Ingredients:

- **1 pound** white fish fillets (such as tilapia or cod)
- **2 tablespoons** olive oil
- **1 teaspoon** cumin
- **1 teaspoon** chili powder
- **Salt and pepper** to taste
- **8 corn tortillas**
- **1 cup** cabbage slaw
- **1/4 cup** lime juice
- **Fresh cilantro** (for garnish)

Instructions:

1. In a bowl, mix olive oil, cumin, chili powder, salt, and pepper. Brush this mixture onto the fish fillets.
2. Preheat the grill to medium heat. Grill the fish for about 3-4 minutes per side until cooked through and flaky.
3. In another bowl, toss cabbage slaw with lime juice and a pinch of salt.
4. Warm the corn tortillas on the grill for about 1 minute on each side. Fill each tortilla with grilled fish and top with slaw. Garnish with fresh cilantro.

Spicy Grilled Cauliflower Steaks

Ingredients:

- **1 large head** cauliflower, sliced into 1-inch thick steaks
- **3 tablespoons** olive oil
- **2 teaspoons** smoked paprika
- **1 teaspoon** cayenne pepper (adjust to taste)
- **Salt and pepper** to taste
- **Fresh cilantro** (for garnish)

Instructions:

1. Preheat the grill to medium heat.
2. In a small bowl, whisk together olive oil, smoked paprika, cayenne pepper, salt, and pepper.
3. Brush both sides of the cauliflower steaks with the spice mixture.
4. Grill the steaks for about 5-7 minutes per side until tender and charred. Garnish with fresh cilantro before serving.

BBQ Meatball Sliders

Ingredients:

- **1 pound** ground beef or turkey
- **1/2 cup** breadcrumbs
- **1/4 cup** grated Parmesan cheese
- **1 egg**
- **1/4 cup** BBQ sauce (plus more for serving)
- **Salt and pepper** to taste
- **Slider buns** (for serving)

Instructions:

1. In a bowl, mix together ground meat, breadcrumbs, Parmesan cheese, egg, BBQ sauce, salt, and pepper until well combined.
2. Preheat the grill to medium heat. Form the mixture into small meatballs.
3. Grill the meatballs for about 8-10 minutes, turning occasionally, until fully cooked.
4. Serve on slider buns with additional BBQ sauce.

Grilled Watermelon Salad

Ingredients:

- **1 small seedless watermelon**, cut into thick wedges
- **1 tablespoon** olive oil
- **Feta cheese**, crumbled (for topping)
- **Fresh mint leaves** (for garnish)
- **Balsamic glaze** (for drizzling)
- **Salt and pepper** to taste

Instructions:

1. Preheat the grill to medium heat.
2. Brush the watermelon wedges lightly with olive oil.
3. Grill the watermelon for about 2-3 minutes on each side until grill marks appear.
4. Arrange on a plate, sprinkle with feta cheese and fresh mint, drizzle with balsamic glaze, and season with salt and pepper.

Grilled Stuffed Peppers

Ingredients:

- **4 bell peppers** (any color)
- **1 cup** cooked quinoa or rice
- **1 can** black beans, rinsed and drained
- **1 cup** corn (fresh, frozen, or canned)
- **1 teaspoon** cumin
- **1 teaspoon** chili powder
- **Salt and pepper** to taste
- **1 cup** shredded cheese (optional)

Instructions:

1. Preheat the grill to medium heat.
2. Cut the tops off the bell peppers and remove the seeds. In a bowl, mix quinoa or rice, black beans, corn, cumin, chili powder, salt, and pepper.
3. Stuff the peppers with the mixture and top with cheese if desired.
4. Wrap the peppers in foil and grill for about 20-25 minutes until the peppers are tender.

Caribbean Jerk Chicken

Ingredients:

- 4 boneless, skinless chicken thighs
- **2 tablespoons** jerk seasoning
- **1 tablespoon** olive oil
- **Juice of 1 lime**
- **Salt** to taste

Instructions:

1. In a bowl, combine jerk seasoning, olive oil, lime juice, and salt. Add the chicken and marinate for at least 30 minutes.
2. Preheat the grill to medium-high heat. Grill the chicken for about 6-7 minutes per side until fully cooked.
3. Let the chicken rest for a few minutes before slicing and serving.

Smoky BBQ Beans

Ingredients:

- **2 cans** navy beans or pinto beans, rinsed and drained
- **1 cup** BBQ sauce
- **1/2 onion**, chopped
- **1 tablespoon** smoked paprika
- **Salt and pepper** to taste

Instructions:

1. In a medium bowl, combine beans, BBQ sauce, chopped onion, smoked paprika, salt, and pepper.
2. Transfer the mixture to a cast-iron skillet or a grill-safe pan.
3. Place on the grill over indirect heat for about 30-40 minutes, stirring occasionally, until heated through and bubbly.

Grilled Shrimp and Vegetable Skewers

Ingredients:

- **1 pound** shrimp, peeled and deveined
- **1 bell pepper**, cut into squares
- **1 zucchini**, sliced
- **1 red onion**, cut into chunks
- **2 tablespoons** olive oil
- **1 teaspoon** garlic powder
- **Salt and pepper** to taste
- **Skewers** (soaked in water if wooden)

Instructions:

1. Preheat the grill to medium-high heat.
2. In a bowl, toss shrimp and vegetables with olive oil, garlic powder, salt, and pepper.
3. Thread shrimp and vegetables onto skewers, alternating as desired.
4. Grill the skewers for about 2-3 minutes per side until shrimp are cooked through and vegetables are tender.

BBQ Chicken Salad

Ingredients:

- **2 cups** cooked chicken, shredded
- **1 cup** BBQ sauce
- **4 cups** mixed greens
- **1 cup** cherry tomatoes, halved
- **1/2 cup** red onion, sliced
- **1 cup** corn (fresh, frozen, or canned)
- **1/2 cup** shredded cheese (optional)

Instructions:

1. In a bowl, mix shredded chicken with BBQ sauce until well coated.
2. In a large salad bowl, combine mixed greens, cherry tomatoes, red onion, corn, and cheese.
3. Top the salad with BBQ chicken and toss to combine. Serve immediately.

Honey Glazed Grilled Carrots

Ingredients:

- **1 pound** baby carrots (or regular carrots, cut into sticks)
- **3 tablespoons** honey
- **2 tablespoons** olive oil
- **1 teaspoon** salt
- **1/2 teaspoon** black pepper
- **Fresh parsley** (for garnish)

Instructions:

1. Preheat the grill to medium heat.
2. In a bowl, whisk together honey, olive oil, salt, and pepper.
3. Toss the carrots in the honey mixture until well coated.
4. Grill the carrots for about 10-15 minutes, turning occasionally, until tender and slightly charred. Garnish with fresh parsley before serving.

Grilled Lobster Tails

Ingredients:

- **4 lobster tails**
- **1/4 cup** melted butter
- **2 tablespoons** lemon juice
- **1 teaspoon** garlic powder
- **Salt and pepper** to taste
- **Lemon wedges** (for serving)

Instructions:

1. Preheat the grill to medium-high heat.
2. Split the lobster tails in half lengthwise and remove any veins.
3. In a bowl, combine melted butter, lemon juice, garlic powder, salt, and pepper.
4. Brush the lobster meat with the butter mixture. Grill the tails flesh-side down for about 5-7 minutes, then flip and grill for an additional 3-5 minutes until cooked through.
5. Serve with lemon wedges.

Chipotle Lime Grilled Corn

Ingredients:

- **4 ears** of corn, husked
- **2 tablespoons** olive oil
- **1 tablespoon** chipotle seasoning
- **Juice of 1 lime**
- **Salt** to taste
- **Fresh cilantro** (for garnish)

Instructions:

1. Preheat the grill to medium-high heat.
2. In a bowl, whisk together olive oil, chipotle seasoning, lime juice, and salt.
3. Brush the corn with the mixture, ensuring it's well coated.
4. Grill the corn for about 10-12 minutes, turning occasionally until charred and tender. Garnish with fresh cilantro before serving.

BBQ Brisket

Ingredients:

- **3 pounds** beef brisket
- **1/4 cup** BBQ rub
- **1 cup** BBQ sauce (for serving)
- **Wood chips** (optional, for smoking)

Instructions:

1. Preheat the grill to medium-low heat, adding wood chips for a smoky flavor if desired.
2. Rub the brisket generously with BBQ rub.
3. Place the brisket on the grill and cook low and slow for about 4-6 hours, maintaining a consistent temperature, until tender.
4. Let the brisket rest for 15 minutes before slicing. Serve with BBQ sauce.

Grilled Pesto Chicken

Ingredients:

- **4 boneless, skinless chicken breasts**
- **1/2 cup** pesto sauce
- **Salt and pepper** to taste
- **Parmesan cheese** (for garnish)

Instructions:

1. Preheat the grill to medium-high heat.
2. Season the chicken breasts with salt and pepper. Coat with pesto sauce.
3. Grill the chicken for about 6-8 minutes per side or until fully cooked.
4. Garnish with grated Parmesan cheese before serving.

Summer Vegetable Platter

Ingredients:

- **1 zucchini**, sliced
- **1 bell pepper**, cut into strips
- **1 red onion**, sliced
- **1 cup** cherry tomatoes
- **2 tablespoons** olive oil
- **Salt and pepper** to taste

Instructions:

1. Preheat the grill to medium heat.
2. In a bowl, toss the vegetables with olive oil, salt, and pepper.
3. Grill the vegetables for about 5-7 minutes, turning occasionally until tender and slightly charred.
4. Serve warm or at room temperature on a platter.

Grilled Sweet Potatoes

Ingredients:

- **2 large sweet potatoes**, cut into 1/2-inch rounds
- **2 tablespoons** olive oil
- **1 teaspoon** paprika
- **Salt and pepper** to taste

Instructions:

1. Preheat the grill to medium heat.
2. In a bowl, toss sweet potato rounds with olive oil, paprika, salt, and pepper.
3. Grill the sweet potatoes for about 5-7 minutes per side until tender and grill marks appear.
4. Serve warm as a side dish.

Honey Mustard Grilled Chicken

Ingredients:

- **4 boneless, skinless chicken thighs**
- **1/4 cup** honey
- **1/4 cup** Dijon mustard
- **1 tablespoon** apple cider vinegar
- **Salt and pepper** to taste

Instructions:

1. In a bowl, whisk together honey, Dijon mustard, apple cider vinegar, salt, and pepper.
2. Marinate the chicken in the mixture for at least 30 minutes.
3. Preheat the grill to medium heat. Grill the chicken for about 6-7 minutes per side until cooked through.
4. Brush with additional marinade during grilling if desired. Serve hot.

Margherita Grilled Pizza

Ingredients:

- **1 pizza dough** (store-bought or homemade)
- **1 cup** fresh mozzarella cheese, sliced
- **1/2 cup** tomato sauce
- **1/4 cup** fresh basil leaves
- **2 tablespoons** olive oil
- **Salt and pepper** to taste

Instructions:

1. Preheat the grill to medium-high heat.
2. Roll out the pizza dough on a lightly floured surface to your desired thickness.
3. Brush one side of the dough with olive oil and place it oil-side down on the grill. Grill for about 2-3 minutes until grill marks form.
4. Flip the dough and spread the tomato sauce over the grilled side. Top with mozzarella slices, salt, and pepper.
5. Close the grill lid and cook for another 4-5 minutes until the cheese is melted and bubbly.
6. Remove from the grill, garnish with fresh basil, slice, and serve.

Teriyaki Grilled Chicken

Ingredients:

- **4 boneless, skinless chicken breasts**
- **1/2 cup** teriyaki sauce
- **2 tablespoons** sesame seeds (for garnish)
- **Sliced green onions** (for garnish)

Instructions:

1. Marinate the chicken breasts in teriyaki sauce for at least 30 minutes (or up to 4 hours in the refrigerator).
2. Preheat the grill to medium heat.
3. Remove the chicken from the marinade and discard any leftover marinade.
4. Grill the chicken for about 6-7 minutes per side until fully cooked and juices run clear.
5. Garnish with sesame seeds and sliced green onions before serving.

Grilled Lemon Herb Potatoes

Ingredients:

- **1.5 pounds** baby potatoes, halved
- **3 tablespoons** olive oil
- **Juice of 1 lemon**
- **2 teaspoons** dried oregano
- **Salt and pepper** to taste
- **Fresh parsley** (for garnish)

Instructions:

1. Preheat the grill to medium heat.
2. In a large bowl, combine olive oil, lemon juice, oregano, salt, and pepper. Add the potatoes and toss to coat.
3. Place the potatoes in a grill basket or wrap in aluminum foil.
4. Grill for about 20-25 minutes, turning occasionally, until tender and lightly charred.
5. Garnish with fresh parsley before serving.

BBQ Cauliflower Bites

Ingredients:

- **1 head** cauliflower, cut into bite-sized florets
- **1/2 cup** BBQ sauce
- **2 tablespoons** olive oil
- **Salt and pepper** to taste
- **Chopped fresh parsley** (for garnish)

Instructions:

1. Preheat the grill to medium heat.
2. In a large bowl, toss the cauliflower florets with olive oil, BBQ sauce, salt, and pepper until well coated.
3. Place the cauliflower in a grill basket or on skewers.
4. Grill for about 15-20 minutes, turning occasionally, until tender and slightly charred.
5. Garnish with chopped parsley before serving.

Grilled Fruit Salad

Ingredients:

- **1 pineapple**, peeled and cut into rings
- **2 peaches**, halved and pitted
- **1 cup** strawberries, hulled
- **1 cup** watermelon, cut into cubes
- **2 tablespoons** honey
- **1 tablespoon** lime juice
- **Fresh mint leaves** (for garnish)

Instructions:

1. Preheat the grill to medium heat.
2. Brush the fruit (pineapple, peaches, and watermelon) lightly with honey and lime juice.
3. Grill the fruit for about 2-3 minutes per side until grill marks appear and the fruit is slightly softened.
4. Remove from the grill and allow to cool slightly. Toss the grilled fruit in a bowl and garnish with fresh mint leaves before serving.

Shrimp and Andouille Sausage Skewers

Ingredients:

- **1 pound** shrimp, peeled and deveined
- **1/2 pound** Andouille sausage, sliced
- **2 tablespoons** olive oil
- **1 tablespoon** Cajun seasoning
- **1 bell pepper**, cut into chunks
- **1 onion**, cut into chunks
- **Skewers** (soaked in water if wooden)

Instructions:

1. Preheat the grill to medium-high heat.
2. In a bowl, combine shrimp, sausage, olive oil, and Cajun seasoning. Toss until well coated.
3. Thread the shrimp, sausage, bell pepper, and onion onto skewers.
4. Grill skewers for about 3-4 minutes per side, until shrimp are pink and cooked through.
5. Serve hot as an appetizer or main dish.

BBQ Chicken Nachos

Ingredients:

- **2 cups** cooked chicken, shredded
- **1 cup** BBQ sauce
- **4 cups** tortilla chips
- **2 cups** shredded cheese (cheddar or Monterey Jack)
- **1/2 cup** sliced jalapeños (optional)
- **1/4 cup** green onions, chopped
- **Sour cream** (for serving)

Instructions:

1. Preheat the grill to medium heat.
2. In a bowl, mix shredded chicken with BBQ sauce until well coated.
3. On a large piece of aluminum foil, layer tortilla chips, BBQ chicken, cheese, and jalapeños.
4. Fold the foil to create a pouch, leaving space for heat circulation.
5. Grill for about 10-15 minutes, until the cheese is melted and bubbly.
6. Carefully open the foil pouch and top with green onions. Serve with sour cream.

Grilled Fajitas

Ingredients:

- **1 pound** flank steak or chicken breasts
- **1 bell pepper**, sliced
- **1 onion**, sliced
- **2 tablespoons** olive oil
- **2 tablespoons** fajita seasoning
- **Flour or corn tortillas** (for serving)
- **Sour cream** and **guacamole** (for serving)

Instructions:

1. Preheat the grill to medium-high heat.
2. Toss the meat, bell pepper, onion, olive oil, and fajita seasoning together in a bowl.
3. Grill the meat for about 5-7 minutes per side, until cooked to your liking. Grill the veggies for about 8-10 minutes, turning occasionally.
4. Remove from the grill and let the meat rest for a few minutes. Slice the meat thinly against the grain.
5. Serve the sliced meat and grilled veggies in tortillas, topped with sour cream and guacamole.

Grilled Honey Garlic Shrimp

Ingredients:

- **1 pound** shrimp, peeled and deveined
- **1/4 cup** honey
- **1/4 cup** soy sauce
- **2 cloves** garlic, minced
- **1 tablespoon** olive oil
- **1 tablespoon** lime juice
- **Skewers** (soaked in water if wooden)

Instructions:

1. In a bowl, whisk together honey, soy sauce, garlic, olive oil, and lime juice.
2. Add the shrimp and marinate for at least 15 minutes.
3. Preheat the grill to medium heat.
4. Thread shrimp onto skewers and discard marinade.
5. Grill the shrimp for about 2-3 minutes per side, until pink and cooked through.
6. Serve hot with a side of rice or a fresh salad.

BBQ Steak Salad

Ingredients:

- **1 pound** steak (flank, sirloin, or ribeye)
- **8 cups** mixed salad greens
- **1 cup** cherry tomatoes, halved
- **1/2 cucumber**, sliced
- **1/4 red onion**, thinly sliced
- **1/4 cup** BBQ sauce (for dressing)
- **Salt and pepper** to taste

Instructions:

1. Preheat the grill to medium-high heat.
2. Season the steak with salt and pepper. Grill for about 4-6 minutes per side for medium-rare, or until desired doneness.
3. Remove from the grill and let rest for a few minutes before slicing.
4. In a large bowl, combine salad greens, cherry tomatoes, cucumber, and red onion.
5. Top with sliced steak and drizzle with BBQ sauce. Toss gently and serve immediately.

www.ingramcontent.com/pod-product-compliance
Lightning Source LLC
LaVergne TN
LVHW081504060526
838201LV00056BA/2927